Animals
Q&A

Can You See Me?

by

SHIRLEY GREENWAY

photographs by

OXFORD SCIENTIFIC FILMS

Ideals Children's Books   Nashville, Tennessee

Published by Ideals Publishing Corporation
Nashville, Tennessee 37214

Printed and bound in the United States of America.

Created and designed by Treld Bicknell.

Library of Congress Cataloging-in-Publication Data

Greenway, Shirley.
Can you see me?/by Shirley Greenway; photographs
by Oxford Scientific Films.
p.   cm.
Summary: Photographs show various animals using
camouflage techniques to remain concealed in their
natural environment, while text provides information
about their survival techniques, habits, and diet.
ISBN 0-8249-8575-3 (lib. bdg.)
ISBN 0-8249-8560-5 (trade pbk.)
1. Camouflage (Biology)—Juvenile literature.
[1. Camouflage (Biology)] I. Oxford Scientific Films.
II. Title. III. Series.
QL767.G74   1992
591.57'2—dc20   92-5215
                                                                    CIP
                                                                    AC

Acknowledgments:
The author and publisher wish to thank the following for permission to reproduce copyright material: **Oxford
Scientific Films** for front cover, back cover, pp. 3, 12, 22, and 26 (Michael Fogden); title page (Konrad Wothe); p. 4
(Keith Porter); p. 5 (Derek Bromhall); pp. 6 and 29 (Richard Packwood); p. 7 (David Cayless); p. 8 (Animals
Animals–Zig Leszczynski); pp. 10-11 (Max Gibbs); p. 13 (Sean Morris); p. 14 (John Cooke); p. 15 (Lloyd Nielson); p. 16
(Stan Osolinski); p. 17 (Judd Cooney); pp. 20-21 (David Thompson); p. 23 (Doug Allan); p. 25 (Alastair Shay); p. 27
(AA–Breck P. Kent); p. 28 (Eyal Bartov); and pp. 18 and 24.

Q. I am a moth,
but what do I look like?

A. The silkmoth opens its wings, revealing two large, black eyespots. This fools birds which are about to swoop—the spots look like the eyes of a snake or a cat rather than an insect mouthful.

Q. I am a spider.

Can you find me?

A. The smooth, round crab spider never builds a web. Instead, it waits patiently for its prey within a flower petal— changing its color to match each new blossom.

I am a lion.

Can you find me?

 Lions hunt more by stealth than speed. With his tawny-colored coat and gently waving mane, this watchful male is almost unseen in the dry, brown grass.

Q. I am a fish.

Can you see me?

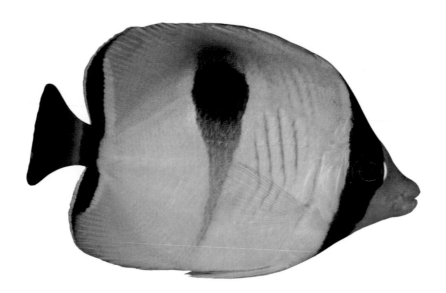

The beautifully named teardrop butterfly fish—with their flattened bodies and large, waving fins—look like butterfly wings as they glide through the water.

Q. I am a katydid.
Can you see me?

A. With its leaflike shape and bright green color, the katydid is almost completely hidden in its surroundings.

Q. I am a bird.

Can you find me?

A. The Australian frogmouth is a *very* strange bird. It feeds at night, catching frogs and other small animals in its huge mouth. During the day it roosts in a dead tree with its eyes closed and its beak held up.

Q. I am a bird too.
Can you see me?

A. The plump ptarmigan (TAR · muh · gen) is the only bird that changes its plumage with the seasons—brown in the summer, gray and white in the fall, and pure white in the winter.

Q. I am an insect.

Can you find me?

A. The stick insect is very hard to spot among the dry leaves and twigs. These large insects are long, brown, and very thin—just like living walking sticks.

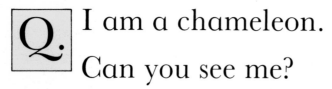 I am a chameleon.
Can you see me?

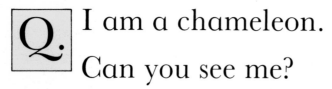 A chameleon (kuh · MEEL · yun) hardly moves at all but changes color to suit its background. There it sits— looking like a leaf, a flower, or the bark of a tree—waiting for insects to come within reach of its long, sticky tongue.

I am a mouse.
Can you see me?

 Harvest mice are so tiny that they can run up and down the stems of ripening grain without being seen. Swinging from a stalk by their tails, the little golden-brown mice gather food with their front paws.

I am a frog.

Can you find me?

 Frogs come in many colors. With their speckled brown skin, leaf frogs can hide among the fallen dry leaves. Brightly colored frogs hide in fresh rainforest leaves and flowers.

Q. I am a cheetah.
Can you see me?

A. The cheetah can run faster than any other animal—but not for very long. Its spotted coat helps to keep it hidden in the dappled shade until likely prey comes in sight.

Animals can hide in many ways:

 The silkmoth has eyespots.

 The fish is marked like butterfly's wings.

 The crab spider looks like a flower.

 The katydid looks like a leaf.

 The lion hides in the grass.

 The frogmouth bird looks li| tree bark.

The ptarmigan changes color with the seasons.

The harvest mouse hides in the grain.

The stick insect appears to be a twig.

The leaf frog is speckled like a leaf.

The chameleon can change color.

The cheetah has a spotted coat.

Index